Animals Under the Ground

Animals Under the Ground

Phyllis J. Perry

Franklin Watts
A Division of Scholastic Inc.
New York • Toronto • London • Auckland • Sydney
Mexico City • New Delhi • Hong Kong
Danbury, Connecticut

For Ann, Claire, Claudia, Elizabeth, Ina, Leslie, and Marie
who love to burrow into books!

Note to readers: Definitions for words in **bold** can be found in the Glossary at the back of this book.

Photographs ©: Animals Animals: 11, 44 (Breck P. Kent), 8 (Raymond A. Mendez), 46 (Leonard Lee Rue III); BBC Natural History Unit: 2, 41 (Jeff Foott), 50 (Andrew Harrington), 16 bottom (Paul Hobson), 26, 42 (Mary Ann McDonald); Brian Kenney: 9; Dembinsky Photo Assoc.: 37 (John Gerlach), 19 (Skip Moody); Peter Arnold Inc.: 33 (John Cancalosi), 30 (C. Allan Morgan), 6 (Hans Pfletschinger), 25 (Michael Sewell); Photo Researchers, NY: 5 left, 15, 18 (Jacana), 53 (Stephen J. Krasemann), cover, 20, 23, 28, 29 (Tom McHugh), 5 right, 34 (Rod Planck), 38 (Leonard Lee Rue III); Visuals Unlimited: 49 (Beth Davidow), 47 (Joe McDonald), 16 top (John Sohlden), 40 (Milton H. Tiernay, Jr.), 12 (William J. Weber).

The photograph on the cover shows an Ord's kangaroo rat. The photograph opposite the title page shows a black-tailed prairie dog.

Library of Congress Cataloging-in-Publication Data

Perry, Phyllis Jean
    Animals Under the Ground / by Phyllis Perry
       p. cm.— (Watts Library)
    Includes bibliographical references and index.
    ISBN 0-531-11759-6 (lib. bdg.)   0-531-16574-4 (pbk.)
    1. Burrowing animals—Juvenile literature. [1. Burrowing animals.] I. Title. II. Series.
QL756.15 .P46 2001
591.56'48 —dc21
                                          00-043601
                                           CIP

© 2001 Franklin Watts, a Division of Scholastic Inc.
All rights reserved. Published simultaneously in Canada.
Printed in the United States of America.
1 2 3 4 5 6 7 8 9 10 R 10 09 08 07 06 05 04 03 02 01

Contents

An earthworm pulls a blade of grass into its burrow.

Chapter One

Life Underground

The next time you go outside, look around for animals. Chances are if you're outdoors—whether you're in wild woodlands or your own backyard—there are many animals nearby. You may not see or hear them, but they are there, perhaps right beneath your feet.

Hundreds of different kinds of creatures live underground, including certain insects, spiders, toads, snakes, earthworms, bears, and even birds. If you dig in moist ground, roll over a large rock, or

These termites are busy in their nest.

carefully examine an uprooted tree, you may discover many underground animals such as grubs, beetles, crickets, worms, or snails. Many ant species live underground in colonies of several hundred thousand members. Even the firefly began its life underground as a member of the beetle family.

Larger animals live underground, too. Rabbits spend a lot of time above ground where they explore and feast on grass and plants. Often, however, they dig short tunnels, and may build underground nests just below the soil's surface. In these fur-lined nests, the rabbits give birth and raise their young.

Many other animals use the underground world as a safe place for their offspring to develop. After mating, a female land turtle digs a hole in which she lays her rubbery-skinned

A Burrowing Owl

Can you imagine a bird that's at home underground? It may seem surprising, but the burrowing owl is a good digger. Often, however, it simply moves into an abandoned burrow dug by other animals, lays its eggs, and hatches its chicks. Only when the chicks are older and stronger do they discover life above ground.

eggs. She covers the nesting spot with debris to conceal it. As soon as the baby turtles crack through their shells, they dig to the surface and begin their active lives above ground.

Adaptations

How do these creatures survive beneath the surface? Many creatures have developed **adaptations** over time that help them to function well in an underground environment. For example, scientists believe that when toads first left the water, they all had webbed feet. When some toads began to dig underground, the toads that had tougher feet were able to dig more easily. Over many years, this kind of digging toad gradually developed a horny growth on its hind feet. This species became known as the spadefoot toad. The process by which such species change over long periods of time is called **evolution**.

Snakes probably evolved from reptiles that had legs and movable eyelids. Over time, they gradually changed. The legs disappeared, leaving long, muscular bodies good for gliding underground. Snakes have adapted to have fixed eyelids, transparent coverings that protect the eye but still permit clear vision.

Hibernation

A number of animals go underground to escape the weather. Some rest underground during the heat of the summer sun. Others **hibernate** during the cold of winter. Chipmunks, which are active in mild weather, curl up and take a long winter sleep in their underground homes. Their young are born in the burrows, and climb out to discover the world above ground when the days become warm again.

An Eastern Chipmunk has curled up for a long winter nap. Many animals hibernate in burrows when the weather turns cold.

Five Burrowers

You've heard about some animals that use underground spaces to protect their young as they grow, and other animals that use burrows to sleep. There are some animals, however, that live a much larger, very active portion of their lives below the ground. Living in burrows has a number of advantages for these creatures. Burrowing animals are protected against the elements. They are safe from predators, except for those that can dig into the burrow after them. This book describes five of these special burrowing **mammals**—the mole, the pocket gopher, the kangaroo rat, the prairie dog, and the badger—that thrive underground.

11

This common mole has soft, velvety fur.

Chapter Two

Meet the Moles

One of the world's most successful burrowing animals is the mole. In Europe, Asia, and North America there are twenty-nine different species of moles. Old World moles are common from Britain to Japan. Moles are also found from coast to coast in the United States.

Although there are many different types of moles, all moles have something in common. They spend almost all of their lives underground in tunnels.

Moles generally build two different

kinds of tunnels. Their surface tunnels are made in light soil, and are used for chasing after prey that's just below the surface. The permanent tunnels are deep burrows, are often arranged in a complicated network, and can be hundreds of feet long. Some of these permanent tunnels are used by several generations of moles.

Moles Up Close

From the tip of its snout to the base of its tail, the average male mole is 5 3/4 inches long (14.6 centimeters) and weighs nearly a quarter of a pound (113 grams). The female mole is slightly smaller. Moles have soft, velvety fur and are brownish-black or mousey-gray in color. A mole's tail is largely bare, and is usually about 1 1/2 inches (4 cm) long. The mole can shake dirt from its fur like a dog shakes off water, by moving muscles just beneath its skin.

The eyes of moles, hidden in their furry coats, have all the right parts—but are not much larger than pinheads! Hunting in the dark under the ground, moles see little. They are not completely blind, though. They can probably detect differences in levels of light.

The mole has no external ears, just a ring of **cartilage** buried in its fur. The mole does not rely solely on that, though, to help it hear to avoid danger and find food. Instead, the mole *feels* sounds, using vibrations picked up by sound-sensitive hairs on its feet and tail. Whiskers on a mole's face, and little bumps on the tip of its snout are very sensitive to

Fashionable Fur

Mole fur was valuable during the early 1900s. It was used for trimming the collars of men's overcoats.

touch. When a worm falls into a mole tunnel, the mole can detect vibrations produced by the worm's movements. It works surprisingly well—in a year, a single mole consumes more than 30 pounds (13 kilograms) of insects, grubs, cutworms, and wireworms. Moles chew up all that food using sharp teeth that fit together like those of a cat or dog. The common mole has thirty-six teeth.

Moles can make sounds, too. They "twitter" when feeding and exploring. When fighting, or frightened, they may give high-pitched squeals.

A European mole has hairless front paws that it can use like shovels to tunnel in the ground.

Molehills are mounds of dirt pushed up to the surface by tunneling moles.

This mole is emerging from its hole. Moles may come to the surface after a rain to hunt earthworms.

Tunneling Technique

When the mole tunnels, it puts its front feet together in front of its nose, and using a movement like the breaststroke of a swimmer, brings its front feet backward and toward the side. When a mole digs just below the surface, it leaves a telltale ridge of dirt on top of the ground. That ridge is formed from soil that is shoved upwards as the mole pushes its body through soft soil. If raised lines of dirt appear one morning in your yard, there may be a mole at work!

In deep burrows, the mole can't just push loose soil upwards. Instead, the loose soil from digging is thrown back along the tunnel. Then the mole turns around and pushes the soil through the tunnel and out to the surface. A mole can excavate 10 pounds (4.5 kg) of soil in 20 minutes, and may dig 70 feet (21 meters) of main tunnel and another 30 feet (9 m) of branching tunnels in a single night. Mounds of dirt pushed up to the surface by tunneling moles are called molehills.

After a rain, earthworms may come to the surface. If the worms are above ground, moles may come to the surface as well to hunt. This above ground expedition is dangerous for the moles. Hawks, owls, foxes, cats, otters, weasels, or skunks may catch the largely defenseless mole above ground.

Shovel Feet

The huge, hairless front paws of a mole turn outward. Like shovels, these paws push back dirt as the mole tunnels.

Raising Their Young

Mole young are usually born in April. During the breeding season, a male mole may travel above ground for up to one-half mile (.8 kilometers) in search of a mate. **Gestation**, the period after mating during which young develop inside the mother's body, lasts for 4 weeks. Most female moles then give birth to their young in an underground nest made of leaves. Some moles, however, are born in fortresses. A fortress is a large molehill up to 3 feet (1 m) high, which contains one or more mole nests and a series of burrows.

Most moles raise a single litter of one to seven babies a year. The young moles are born blind, pink, and naked, but they grow quickly. At birth, they measure 1 1/2 inches (4 cm) long, and weigh only an eighth of an ounce (3.5 g). When they are about 10 days old, young moles grow a light gray coat of fur. Their eyes open on the twenty-second day, but they're still not ready for life on their own. The mother mole feeds her young with her milk for a month after they are born. She may leave her young alone for 2 hours or more while she hunts for food. After 3 weeks, they are almost adult size. They will be full grown and on their own by the time they are 6 weeks old.

Moles sometimes search above ground, collecting prey among grass and litter. A mole will eat half its own weight in a single day.

Three Long Meals a Day

A typical earth day seems like a "three day" cycle for a mole. Moles run on a schedule of eating for 3 hours, then sleeping for 5 hours, and then eating again. Where does the food for those long meals come from? The tunnels of moles are like pit traps. Worms and insects fall in, and the mole hunts them down by running along the burrows. Common underground foods include slugs, snails, crickets, spiders, insect larvae, and earthworms.

Moles may also feed above ground, collecting prey among grass and litter. Moles get all the moisture they need from their food supply, so they don't need to drink water. A mole will eat half its own weight, over 1 1/2 ounces (50 g), in 24 hours.

Some Strange Moles

Although all moles have much in common, there are also features that help to distinguish one kind of mole from another. Their appearance, food preferences, and tunnel-building habits can be very different.

The star-nosed mole has a nose that is divided at the end into a fringe of 22 touch-sensitive tentacles. This mole waves them around as it hunts for its favorite food, the earthworm.

The shrew mole, which lives in the western part of the United States, is the smallest of all the moles. It lacks the large front feet that other moles have. In addition, its fur does not have the soft, velvety quality of other mole fur, and it is more slender in build.

One group of moles, called the desmans, lives in southern Europe and what was once the Soviet Union. This mole likes the water! A desman has waterproof fur, webbed feet, and a flat tail. The desman pokes its snout above water, using it like a snorkel for breathing while it swims.

A star-nosed mole has a most unusual nose. At the end is a fringe made up of 22 tentacles, which it waves as it hunts for earthworms.

A pocket gopher peeks out from its hole.

Chapter Three

Pocket Gophers

Among the burrowers are several kinds of animals called pocket gophers. Pocket gophers are found only in the Western Hemisphere, and are most abundant in the western United States and Mexico. Like many burrowers, they are rodents. The pocket gophers are closely related to the squirrel and the prairie dog.

The pocket gopher gets its first name from two fur-lined pouches on the outside of its cheeks. These pocket-like pouches extend all the way back to the pocket gopher's shoulders, and can be used to carry food such as seeds, grasses, bark, roots, or acorns. The word gopher comes from the French word *gaufre*, which means "honeycomb." Early French settlers noticed that pocket gophers dig tunnels so extensively that they make a honeycomb of the ground.

The Pocket Gopher Up Close

Pocket gophers vary greatly in size. The common western pocket gopher is only 5 inches (13 cm) long. One of the largest of the pocket gophers, though, is over three times as long, measuring 18 inches (46 cm) in length! Though the size of different kinds of pocket gophers varies, they look much alike.

Pocket gophers are thick-set and seem to lack a neck. Their bodies are covered with dense, soft, brownish-gray fur. Their legs are short, and their forelegs have strong, curved claws.

They are nearsighted, with small, weak eyes. Their tiny, rounded ears are hidden under the skin. Like the mole, a pocket gopher is well suited to life underground. Pocket gophers have developed ways to protect their sensing organs. Dirt does not get in the eyes of a pocket gopher because it has

Open Wide

The mouth of a pocket gopher is very strange. Its upper jaw sticks out beyond its lower jaw. The upper **incisor** teeth are moved forward, in front of the upper lip! The fur-lined lips form a tight seal over its mouth, which is a small hole above the lower incisors.

tight-fitting eyelids. Its ears have valves that close. Sensitive hairs that grow along its mouth, nose, and body enable the pocket gopher to feel its way around in the dark.

The pocket gopher has a short, almost hairless tail with a sensitive tip. This tip helps the pocket gopher feel its way when it is moving backward through tunnels.

Honeycombs in the Ground

Except during mating season, pocket gophers live alone. It is typical for only one adult to live in each burrow system. To build its burrow, the pocket gopher digs with its claws, pushing the dirt backward into a mound. When it comes up against hard dirt or a rock, the gopher uses its teeth.

While tunneling, the gopher gets rid of excess dirt by making openings to the surface at regular intervals. The gopher pushes the loose soil through an opening, and then plugs up the opening again.

The pocket gopher digs with its claws. In its burrow, there are a number of special rooms.

In its burrow, the pocket gopher builds a number of rooms. One room is used as a toilet. Another room is the pocket gopher's nest. The nest room is lined with finely shredded leaves and grass. Eight or nine rooms are used for storage of tubers and roots. Since the pocket gopher does not hibernate, it depends on all that stored food to live through the winter months when vegetation is scarce.

Raising Their Young

In spring, the male pocket gopher leaves his territory and goes to court a female. Once he finds a willing partner, they mate in her den. The male then usually returns to his den, although sometimes males stay and help the females with the raising of the young for a few weeks.

The female gopher lays in a supply of extra food to help her feed her young. Three weeks after mating, she gives birth to a litter of blind, naked baby pocket gophers. A litter may contain as few as one baby to as many as twelve, though typically a litter ranges from two to six young. Newborn pocket gophers are covered in pink skin. Later, they will grow brown fur.

The mother nurses the young as they grow. In about a month, their eyes and ears open. When the young pocket gophers are about 2 months old, the mother opens the plug that seals the burrow. The little ones crawl above ground. They are now on their own to dig new burrows, or to find an empty burrow elsewhere and move in.

Gopher Gourmet

The pocket gopher, which eats only plants, sometimes comes above ground to search for green vegetation. Often it tunnels just below the surface of the ground to hack off chunks from the roots of plants. It uses its cutting teeth, or incisors, to gnaw food. It stashes the food it finds in its cheek pouches.

Safe back in its burrow, the pocket gopher empties its pouches. It uses its front feet to squeeze on the pouches from the back to front, spilling its food out onto the ground. Then the pocket gopher sorts and stores its food in its storage chambers. It gets all the water that it needs from the plants it eats.

A Dangerous Time

While it is above ground, the pocket gopher faces danger from predators such as snakes, hawks, and foxes.

Kangaroo rats have fur-lined cheek pouches in which they store plant seeds.

Chapter Four

Kangaroo Rats

Several species of animals called kangaroo rats are found in the southwestern United States. The kangaroo rats are closely related to pocket gophers, and are part of the same family as pocket mice and kangaroo mice. Both families have fur-lined cheek pouches. How did this small rodent get its name? The kangaroo rat often travels by hopping along on its large hind feet—much like a kangaroo.

Kangaroo rats primarily eat the seeds of desert and grassland plants. They are able to survive with very little or no water. They can convert the dry seeds that they eat into the water they need. They don't sweat, and don't pant when they are warm. In fact, they have no sweat glands at all! Both those special adaptations allow them to conserve water.

Though kangaroo rats live mainly in very dry or desert habitats, the air in their underground burrows stays moist and humid. They are **nocturnal**, coming out of their burrows only at night. That's another adaptation so that they don't lose too much precious water in the hot desert sun.

Meet the Kangaroo Rat

The kangaroo rat is a dainty, fawn-colored animal, with large brown eyes, and thin, pink ears. Its eyes are set well back on the sides of its head so that it can see things above it, as well as things in front and below. A full-grown kangaroo rat weighs about 4 ounces (113 g). It measures 15 inches (38 cm) from the tip of its nose to the tip of its 9-inch (23-cm) tail.

A white stripe runs down the outside of its brown fur. Its throat and breast are white, and it has a long tail that has two white stripes and ends in a

Getting Clean in the Dirt

Kangaroo rats enjoy taking dust baths. The dust smothers fleas, mites, and other parasites that bother kangaroo rats.

28

tuft of fur. It has large, strong hind feet with stiff hairs on the bottom and clawlike toes. These toes and its incisor teeth are excellent for digging. However, the kangaroo rat isn't strong all over. It has small, weak, front legs. Its forefeet are tiny, rounded, and pinkish-white.

When the kangaroo rat jumps, it holds its forepaws curled up against its chest. The kangaroo rat's long, sturdy tail serves both as support and balance. Like the pocket gopher, the kangaroo rat has two outer, fur-lined cheek pouches in which it stores food. Kangaroo rats make long, drawn-out musical

The eyes of a kangaroo rat are set well back on the sides of its head so that it can look for enemies above as well as ahead and below.

This kangaroo rat is plugging up the entrance to its burrow.

notes at night that sound like a bird song, with high-pitched trills and deeper notes.

Air-Conditioned Tunnels

The kangaroo rat survives its desert environment by living in underground tunnels. Outside, there may be a blazing hot sun, but the temperature in a burrow stays a bearable 46 to 85 degrees Fahrenheit (8 to 29 degrees Celsius).

The kangaroo rat digs its burrow with its tiny front paws, shooting loose earth out behind it between its hind legs. The burrow is usually 2 or 3 feet (0.6 to 0.9 m) deep. The nine or more entrances and exits are located around prickly thistles, soapweed, or Spanish bayonet plants. These sharp plants discourage predators from digging into the burrow entrances.

A burrow may contain three levels of tunnels. That maze of tunnels leads to a central chamber with a small air shaft. The kangaroo rat plugs the opening to the main chamber each time it leaves. A lizard or other creature wandering the tunnels might pass by and walk straight out another tunnel, without ever finding the main chamber.

The main chamber is about 5 or 6 inches (14 cm) high and measures 12 by 8 inches (30 cm by 20 cm). In a corner is a mass of interlaced, spiny grasses, which conceals the entrance to the nest. The nest is made of fine grasses, weed silk, and feathers.

Other hidden passages from the main chamber slant down to deep storage rooms, which are cool enough so that seeds stored in them do not sprout. Another tunnel leads to a room used as a toilet. There are also false tunnels leading to plugged up blind alleys.

Raising Their Young

Most of the time, a kangaroo rat lives alone. Mating takes place in April and August, and a litter of two to four babies is born about 4 weeks later. The young are born hairless, and their eyes and ears are closed. The mother kangaroo rat stays and nurses her babies for 15 days eating stored food during this time.

Sometimes an animal like a badger finds the burrow. A badger can dig quickly and will eat mother and babies. If the mother kangaroo rat hears an enemy approach, she picks up

Thumper

If a kangaroo rat hears danger, it stamps its big hind feet to frighten away an unwelcome intruder.

one of her babies, escapes through a back tunnel, hides, and waits until danger passes.

When they are 3 months old, the young kangaroo rats are ready to leave the nest. The mother kangaroo rat unplugs the burrow and gently nudges the babies out into the world.

Food

The kangaroo rat comes out of its burrow at night to forage for food. It gathers seeds using its incisors to cut plants or roots. The kangaroo rat packs the food in cheek pouches and then carries it to storage chambers in the burrows. Each kind of seed is stored separately.

In the desert springtime, kangaroo rats eat plant stems, fungi, and seeds. They may live their lifespan of 3 or 4 years without ever seeking water from pools or streams. Their bodies are specially adapted to create water from the food the kangaroo rat eats.

During digestion, the kangaroo rat's body breaks down starches in the seeds, releasing hydrogen and oxygen. These chemicals combine to make water in the animal's digestive system. Even though it does not drink, this little creature has a body which is 65 percent water. That's about the same water content found in many animals that can drink whenever they want! Although food may be scarce outside, the kangaroo rat does not hibernate through the winter. All through the cold months it eats seeds that it has stored in its burrow during the summer months.

Packed Pouch

Each kangaroo rat pouch holds about a teaspoonful of seeds.

Enemies

A kangaroo rat has many enemies. Badgers and snakes may attack it in its burrow. At night, as it hunts for food, a horned owl may swoop down and carry a kangaroo rat away. A fox or a coyote may also discover the kangaroo rat.

One of the enemies of the kangaroo rat is the gopher snake. Badgers, foxes, and coyotes also eat kangaroo rats.

A Clever Fighter

Even though it has tiny weak front feet, if threatened, a kangaroo rat is a clever fighter. First, it turns its back toward the enemy, balances on its short front legs, and with its strong hind legs kicks dirt at the face of its enemy. Then the kangaroo rat rushes to its burrow and blocks the entrance with dirt.

Standing at alert, this black-tailed prairie dog is looking and listening for any possible danger.

Chapter Five

Prairie Dogs

French explorers called them *petits chiens*, or little dogs. However, prairie dogs are not related to dogs, or any members of the canine family. Other observers called them barking squirrels or prairie squirrels. Those people were on the right track. Prairie dogs are rodents. They do belong to the squirrel family. They are close relatives to marmots, ground squirrels, and chipmunks.

Prairie dogs live only in North America. They are found in northern Mexico and southern Canada, but most live in the Great Plains and Rocky Mountain regions of the United States.

A typical prairie dog is a foot long (30 cm) and weighs 1 to 3 pounds (450 g to 1.4 kg). It has very short legs. The eyes of prairie dogs are located high in their heads allowing them to check for danger from the sky. They have excellent hearing and are very alert.

The prairie dog's coarse fur is a buff color that blends in well with its surroundings. A prairie dog has a short black or white tail.

Digging Dogs

Prairie dogs dig tunnels using their long, sharp claws. There are a variety of rooms in a typical prairie dog burrow, including a toilet, sleeping chambers, storage rooms, and a nursery. The nest chamber is filled with grass to make it soft.

A foot-high, cone-shaped mound at the surface lets most rainwater run down its sides and seep into the earth at the mound's base instead of flooding the burrow. Air flows from one end of the burrow to the other, always coming out the dome of the mound. From the top of the mound, an entrance shaft dives straight down for 5 to 15 feet (1.5 m to 4.6 m). This leads to a main, horizontal tunnel, which may run for 80 feet (24 m). There is also a long back tunnel with an escape hole.

Just below the entrance, the tunnel widens into a ledge. Before leaving the safety of its burrow, the prairie dog stops on the ledge and listens. If all is quiet, the prairie dog climbs outside and sits upright near the small mound, close to the burrow opening.

*These black-tailed prairie dogs
live not far from a famous rock
formation known as Devil's Tower.*

Visitors Drop In

Birds called horned larks may come inside the entrance of a prairie dog burrow hunting insects.

A prairie dog town may contain thirty mounds with connecting tunnels. A group living in the town is called a **coterie**. A typical coterie is made up of one or two males, one of which acts as chief, several females, and their young.

Unwelcome Guests

Prairie dogs are the primary food for a large number of birds and animals. They must be constantly alert to danger on the ground, from the sky, and even from within their burrows. Enemies of the prairie dogs include badgers, black-footed ferrets, bobcats, owls, foxes, weasels, coyotes, and snakes.

Rattlesnakes may enter the prairie dog burrows seeking young prairie dogs to eat. At the first sign of an intruder, prairie dogs will bark to alert the others to the danger. Sometimes prairie dogs will block the opening and the escape

A hungry coyote digs quickly trying to capture a prairie dog for dinner.

entrance to a burrow, trapping the snake inside where it may die from lack of air and food.

A rattlesnake may also move into a burrow seeking a warm place in which to hibernate during the cold winter. One snake may be joined by others, and several of them may tangle and curl up together and hibernate until spring in a nesting chamber.

Raising Their Young

Prairie dogs mate in January and February. The male joins the female and her offspring in the burrow and stays for several days before leaving and returning to his own burrow nearby.

After the parents mate, the young develop in the female for 28 to 32 days. In March or April, a litter of two to ten pups is born in a nesting chamber lined with soft grass. The newborn pups are tiny and helpless. They lack fur, and their eyes are closed. Each pup weighs about half an ounce (14 g). As with all mammals, the mother prairie dog nurses her young.

The pups grow rapidly, and their eyes open in about 2 weeks. After 6 or 7 weeks, the young are ready to go above ground to search for food.

A mother prairie dog takes care of her young in spring and summer. Before winter, the mother turns over the burrow to her offspring, and she digs another den.

Before winter, the mother turns the burrow over to her offspring and digs another den. Her mate or other members of her clan may help her with the digging. Sometime during the following spring, the year-old young pair up and leave to make homes of their own. They may go only a short distance to build a new prairie dog town.

Prairie Dog Dinner

Prairie dogs hunt for green plants. The most common prairie grass is blue grama grass. Other favorite foods are bluestem and pepper grass. Usually the prairie dogs sit on their hind feet and hold these leafy weeds in their front paws to eat.

During the warm months, prairie dogs may also eat grasshoppers, beetles, and cutworms. In the fall, when the grass turns brown and dry, prairie dogs dig up roots to eat. They also claw at low cactus plants and eat the soft insides, taking care to avoid the spines.

Prairie dogs are well equipped for a diet of grasses, with long incisors and broad molars. They have large stomachs, and parts of the starchy food they eat is converted by chemical action into water, allowing prairie dogs to go for long periods without drinking.

During the winter, there is little food. The prairie dogs eat lots during the summer to build up a store of fat, which helps them to survive during lean times.

Pucker Up

Prairie dogs communicate with each other through chirps, barks, and whistles. Prairie dogs sometimes seem to kiss. They approach each other, meet, touch noses, and bare and touch their teeth. This helps prairie dogs from the same coterie to recognize one another. After "kissing," prairie dogs from the same coterie may groom one another. Prairie dogs from different coteries, however, may run away or fight. Prairie dogs also communicate with a wag or flick of their tails.

When prairie dogs meet, they approach each other, touch noses, and bare and touch their teeth. This is the way prairie dogs from the same coterie recognize each other.

Settling the West

When the first settlers reached the prairie states, about four hundred million prairie dogs lived there.

The North American badger has a short neck and a broad, flat head. It has a white stripe that extends from its nose to its shoulder and may continue down its back.

Chapter Six

Badgers

Badgers belong to a group of mammals that includes skunks, weasels, and otters. True badgers are classified in six separate species, found in Europe, Asia, Africa, and North America. There are many kinds of badgers, including the North American badger, European badger, hog badger, stink badger, honey badger, and ferret badger.

Badgers are rarely seen during the day. If you do see one, however, stay clear! Whatever their age and size, badgers can be fearful adversaries. They have thick front claws and razor-sharp teeth combined with a jaw that can lock shut when it bites. Unlike the pocket gopher, badgers are **carnivorous**, or meat-eaters.

The North American Badger

Only one badger lives on the North American continent. Appropriately, it's called the North American badger. It is found from northern Alberta to southern Mexico, and from the Pacific Ocean to as far east as Ohio.

The North American badger has a short neck, a broad flat head, and a muscular flat body with short stout legs. Its forefeet are partly webbed. These badgers weigh between 8 and 26 pounds (3.6 kg to 11.8 kg), and are between 16 and 28 inches (41 cm to 71 cm) long. They have fluffy tails that are 4 to 6 inches (10 cm to 15 cm) in length.

Badgers are meat-eaters. They belong to the group of mammals that includes skunks, weasels, and otters.

A North American badger's upper body is reddish-brown or grayish. There is a conspicuous white stripe from nose to shoulder, and in some species the stripe may continue all the way to the rump. Badgers make pig-like grunts and hiss when they are angry.

An adult North American badger has thirty-four sharp teeth. Badgers have rather poor vision but excellent hearing and a good sense of smell. Most badgers normally live to about a dozen years of age.

Except for the mating season, boars (males) and sows (females) live alone. The badger's burrow is not much more than a hole in the ground leading to a long tunnel that may be 30 feet (9 m) in length.

Raising Their Young

North American badgers mate in the summer. Each spring, the female digs a nesting burrow where she gives birth to one to four pups. The sow's underground den may be as much as 8 feet (2.4 m) deep, and is often in an area where there is thick brush to hide it from predators.

The badger pups are blind and helpless for their first month of life. The mother nurses them and keeps them warm. The young are covered in puppy fur, which will grow by summer into an adult coat. As the young grow bigger, the sow leaves the burrow to hunt.

After 2 months, the pups spend more time outside, but not alone. Because of the danger from predators, the mother badger must be watchful. By late summer, when the pups are 3 or 4 months old, they are old enough to take care of themselves, and the group breaks up.

On the Hunt

This badger is digging for its prey. Earth-worms are its favorite food, but badgers also eat things such as prairie dogs, mice, lizards, snails, acorns, grains, and berries.

Badgers are most active at night. They use a keen sense of smell and hearing to locate their prey. Depending on location, the primary prey of North American badgers may be mice, pocket gophers, kangaroo rats, ground squirrels, prairie dogs, or cottontails.

In summer, badgers eat insects, including crickets, beetles, grasshoppers, and caterpillars. They will also raid wasps' and

hornets' nests. A badger can even kill and eat rattlesnakes, and its thick fur prevents a snake's fangs from injecting venom into its bloodstream.

A badger does not drink. It gets all the moisture it needs from the foods it eats.

The European Badger

European badgers are found in Europe, in northern, cooler parts of Asia, and in Japan. They have stocky bodies that measure 3 feet (1 m) from the tip of the nose to the end of the stumpy, 4-inch (10-cm) long tail. European badgers weigh between 25 and 35 pounds (11.3 kg to 15.8 kg). The boars are somewhat heavier than the sows. These badgers have a dark gray body and a whitish head with a black stripe on either side that runs through the eye and ear.

Beware of Badgers

Badgers are fierce fighters. If cornered, a badger turns on its back and rips its attacker with teeth and claws.

Like the North American badger, European badgers have strong jaws that lock. European badgers have thirty-eight teeth. The **canines**, or tearing teeth, are very prominent.

The European badger is noisy. It purrs, growls, hisses, snarls, and even screams. The North American badger, on the other hand, rarely uses its voice except during a fight.

Tunnel Towns

European badgers use both their front and back legs for digging tunnels. The front legs are the most powerful, and the front claws are thick and up to 1 inch (2.5 cm) long.

European badgers live in clans of about ten animals. They dig their **setts**, or towns, in sandy soil near fields and pastures.

Winter Naps

Badgers take winter naps. During their naps, the animals enter a state of **torpor**. This is not as deep a sleep as hibernation, but the badger's body temperature drops, and its heart rate slows down.

When outdoor temperatures rise, the badger stirs. The badger goes above ground and hunts, but when it gets too cold, the badger returns to its burrow to nap again.

A sett may be two or three stories deep with tunnels leading to sleeping chambers and nurseries.

Burrows may be used for a hundred years or more. These passageways, which may extend 100 feet (30 m) may have forty or fifty entrances. The burrows are also air-conditioned. Small holes, placed in tunnels near the surface, act as vents.

Raising Their Young

Eurasian badgers mate for life. Their mating season is from midsummer to early autumn. Before the young are born, the boars move to another part of the sett.

The four or five cubs in each litter are blind. They're furry above, but are hairless on their underparts. The cubs measure about 4 to 5 inches (10 to 13 cm) long. Each weighs 3 ounces (85 g).

When the babies are old enough, they come out of the burrow and begin to explore. Usually by autumn, the cubs leave to dig setts of their own.

Not a Picky Eater

In summer and fall, European badgers hunt at night and fatten up on their favorite food, earthworms. They can eat several hundred worms in a few hours.

European badgers also eat rabbits, voles, lizards, grubs, grains, snails, fruits, and insects. When available, they will also eat acorns, berries, bulbs, fungi, and grasses.

Some people consider prairie dogs to be a great nuisance. These men are on patrol to trap prairie dogs.

Chapter Seven

An Uncertain Future

The future is uncertain for these burrowers. Humans consider many tunneling animals to be pests. Much of the information written about these animals explains how to shoot, trap, or poison them.

However, many people don't realize that these animals do have some economic value. Prairie dogs and moles aerate and enrich soil with their digging and droppings. They eat many pests that destroy agricultural crops. Badgers keep down the rodent population.

The burrowers can cause problems for humans, though. Moles, prairie dogs, and badgers are especially unpopular in farming communities. Sometimes horses stumble into burrow holes, injuring themselves and their riders. Farm machinery can be damaged or broken by running into mounds and burrows. Crops may be harmed as the animals dig and forage.

After World War I, widespread poisoning of prairie dogs began. Conservationists feared that the prairie dog might be wiped out. Prairie dog populations are currently just 1 percent of what they used to be.

Not all the threats to the burrowers are deliberate. As towns and cities have grown, people have built homes and businesses on the habitat of these animals, greatly shrinking the range where these animals can successfully live.

In spite of these problems, it appears that the population of North American badgers is currently growing. Agriculture continues to attract squirrels and mice that eat plant crops and seeds. In turn, the squirrels and mice support a healthy badger population. What may happen when more agricultural land is replaced by urban centers, however, is unclear.

Many prairie dog populations are threatened. Human land development is a significant threat to prairie dog towns. Homes and shopping centers are taking over once vacant fields. In some places, though, prairie dog colonies are being moved to open space lands. In parks in the plains states, prairie dogs are protected and continue to thrive.

The lives of the burrowers are interdependent. Badgers depend on prairie dogs and kangaroo rats for their food supply. The black-footed ferret, one of the rarest mammals in the world, relies on prairie dogs for over 90 percent of its dietary needs. When one animal population is threatened, so are the others that depend on it.

In some cases petitions have been presented asking the government to protect these animals under the Endangered Species Act. Various agencies have taken up the cause of protection and preservation. However, only time will tell how many of the burrowers will survive.

As people move onto open stretches of land to build homes, many burrowing animals lose their natural habitat lands.

Glossary

adaptations—adjustments or modifications of animal bodies or behaviors to fit environmental conditions

canines—large, pointed teeth just behind the front teeth

carnivorous—meat-eating

cartilage—transparent or elastic animal tissue like a soft bone. The tip of your nose contains cartilage.

coterie—a group of prairie dogs that inhabit a prairie dog town

evolution—the process through which species change slowly over generations, developing specialized physical characteristics or behaviors

gestation—the period in which young are carried in the mother's uterus

hibernate—to pass the winter in a state of deep sleep

incisors—the teeth at the front of the jaw

mammals—warm-blooded animals with hair or fur, the females of which produce milk to feed their young

nocturnal—active at night

setts—tunnel-towns used by European badgers

torpor—a dormant, sluggish state

vibrations—the periodic motion of something

To Find Out More

Books

Bailey, Jill. *Discovering Shrews, Moles & Voles*. New York: The Bookwright Press, 1989.

Casey, Denise. *The Friendly Prairie Dog*. New York: Dodd, Mead & Co., 1987.

Dewey, Jennifer Owings. *The Creatures Underneath*. Santa Fe: Red Crane Books, 1994.

Johnson, Annabel. *I Am Leaper*. New York: Scholastic Inc., 1990.

Minta, Kathryn A. *The Digging Badger*. New York: Dodd, Mead & Company, 1985.

Stuart, Gene S. *Towns Down Underground.* National Geographic Society. 1991.

Videos

Cubs and Kittens
Fort Collins, CO: Adventure Productions
Distributed by Twin Tower Enterprises, Inc. 1990
1 videocassette, 30 minutes.
A close-up look at young animals including the badger.

Mole's Christmas
BMG Entertainment International
New York: BMG Video, 1996
1 videocassette, 26 min.
Adapted from *The Wind in the Willows.*

Organizations and Online Sites

The Mammal Society
http://www.abdn.ac.uk/mammal/mole.htm
15 Cloisters House
8 Battersea Park Road
London, England SW8 4BG
Provides information on various animals including the mole.

Rocky Mountain Animal Defense

http://www.rmad.org

2525 Arapahoe, #E4-335

Boulder, CO 80302

The purpose of this group is to help eliminate the human-imposed suffering of animals in the Rocky Mountain region.

Science Frontiers #88, July-August 1993

http://www.science-frontiers.com/sf088/sf088b07.htm

Provides useful information on the star-nosed mole.

Steve Jackson's Brockwatch Badger Pages

http://www.badgers.org.uk/brockwatch/3taxid1.html

Discusses conservation issues surrounding the hunting of the American badger.

Steve Jackson's Brockwatch Badger Pages

http://www.badgers.org.uk/brockwatch/7idsett.html

Explains how to identify badger setts.

A Note on Sources

In doing research, I believe it is important to use a wide variety of resources. First I read on the topic at my local library, using books that I find through the computerized card catalogue. After I have some general information, I speak with a reference librarian and ask for advice on where I might find additional data. This usually results in calling on the services of interlibrary loan collections.

I read specific articles as well as books of general interest. Useful information for this book was available in reports and journals such as *Journal of Range Management, Proceedings of the Conference for Organization and Practice of Vertebrate Pest Control, Environmental Management*, and documents prepared for the U.S. Fish and Wildlife Service. I also research the topic on the Internet.

Local agencies can sometimes provide information. The Rocky Mountain Animal Defense, located in Boulder, Colorado, provided me with a Prairie Dog Action Pack.

When possible, I make firsthand observations by visiting animals in the wild. I have observed prairie dog colonies in Boulder County where I live and in parks in several western states.

—*Phyllis J. Perry*

Index

Numbers in *italics* indicate illustrations.

About the Author

Phyllis J. Perry has worked as an elementary schoolteacher and principal and has written over forty books for teachers and young people. Her most recent books for Franklin Watts are *Bats: The Amazing Upside-Downers*, *Crafty Canines: Coyotes, Foxes & Wolves*, and *Freshwater Giants*. She did her undergraduate work at the University of California, Berkeley and received a doctorate in Curriculum and Instruction from the University of Colorado. Dr. Perry lives with her husband, David, in Boulder, Colorado, where they enjoy the wildflowers, birds, and animals of the Rocky Mountains.